DATE DUE

D R			

DEMCO 38-297

SPORTS GREAT

REBECCA LOBO

SPORTS GREAT

SPORTS GREAT CHARLES BARKLEY REVISED EDITION
0-7660-1004-X/ Macnow

SPORTS GREAT LARRY BIRD
0-89490-368-3/ Kavanagh

SPORTS GREAT MUGGSY BOGUES
0-89490-876-6/ Rekela

SPORTS GREAT KOBE BRYANT
0-7660-1264-6/ Macnow

SPORTS GREAT PATRICK EWING
0-89490-369-1/ Kavanagh

SPORTS GREAT KEVIN GARNETT
0-7660-1263-8/ Macnow

SPORTS GREAT ANFERNEE HARDAWAY
0-89490-758-1/ Rekela

SPORTS GREAT JUWAN HOWARD
0-7660-1065-1/ Savage

SPORTS GREAT MAGIC JOHNSON REVISED AND EXPANDED
0-89490-348-9/ Haskins

SPORTS GREAT MICHAEL JORDAN REVISED EDITION
0-89490-978-9/ Aaseng

SPORTS GREAT JASON KIDD
0-7660-1001-5/ Torres

SPORTS GREAT KARL MALONE
0-89490-599-6/ Savage

SPORTS GREAT REGGIE MILLER
0-89490-874-X/ Thornley

SPORTS GREAT ALONZO MOURNING
0-89490-875-8/ Fortunato

SPORTS GREAT DIKEMBE MUTOMBO
0-7660-1267-0/ Torres

SPORTS GREAT HAKEEM OLAJUWON REVISED EDITION
0-7660-1268-9/ Knapp

SPORTS GREAT SHAQUILLE O'NEAL REVISED EDITION
0-7660-1003-1/ Sullivan

SPORTS GREAT SCOTTIE PIPPEN
0-89490-755-7/ Bjarkman

SPORTS GREAT MITCH RICHMOND
0-7660-1070-8/ Grody.

SPORTS GREAT DAVID ROBINSON REVISED EDITION
0-7660-1077-5/ Aaseng

SPORTS GREAT DENNIS RODMAN
0-89490-759-X/ Thornley

SPORTS GREAT JOHN STOCKTON
0-89490-598-8/ Aaseng

SPORTS GREAT ISIAH THOMAS
0-89490-374-8/ Knapp

SPORTS GREAT CHRIS WEBBER
0-7660-1069-4/ Macnow

SPORTS GREAT DOMINIQUE WILKINS
0-89490-754-9/ Bjarkman

For Other *Sports Great Titles* call:
(800) 398-2504

REBECCA LOBO

Jeff Savage

—SPORTS GREAT BOOKS—

Enslow Publishers, Inc.

40 Industrial Road	PO Box 38
Box 398	Aldershot
Berkeley Heights, NJ 07922	Hants GU12 6BP
USA	UK

http://www.enslow.com

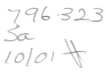
Library of Congress Cataloging-in-Publication Data

Savage, Jeff, 1961–
    Sports Great Rebecca Lobo / Jeff Savage.
       p. cm. — (Sports great books)
    Includes index.
    ISBN 0-7660-1466-5
    1. Lobo, Rebecca—Juvenile literature. 2. Basketball players—United States—
Biography—Juvenile literature. [1. Lobo, Rebecca. 2. Basketball players.
3. Women—Biography.] I. Title: Rebecca Lobo. II. Title. III. Series.
 GV884.L6 S28 2001
 796.323'092—dc21
                                  00-010866

Printed in the United States of America

10 9 8 7 6 5 4 3 2 1

Illustration Credits: Connecticut Women's Basketball, pp. 28, 31, 36, 38, 43,
46; WNBA Enterprises/Bill Baptist, p. 11; WNBA Enterprises/Jennifer
Pottheiser, p. 13; WNBA Enterprises/Nathaniel S. Butler, pp. 9, 15, 18, 20, 49,
58, 61; WNBA Enterprises/Ray Amati, p. 59; WNBA Enterprises/Robert
Mora, p. 25; WNBA Enterprises/Rocky Widner, p. 53.

Cover Illustration: Greg Shamus, NBA Photos

Contents

Chapter 1

A Winner

Rebecca Lobo looked up at the scoreboard hanging from the pinwheel ceiling at New York's Madison Square Garden and read the score: New York Liberty, 17 and Los Angeles Sparks, 17. Lobo knew her Liberty had to win this game. With a 14–10 record late in the season, the Liberty were battling to make the 1998 Women's National Basketball Association (WNBA) playoffs. The Sparks were out of the playoff hunt, but with superstar center Lisa Leslie, they were never out of a game.

Lobo could feel the electricity in the air as more than eighteen thousand fans—the largest crowd of the season— buzzed with excitement. Lobo decided right then to do all she could to short-circuit the Sparks. First, she stepped out and drilled a jumper from the baseline. Next, she rose high to force Leslie to shoot an air ball. Then she made a deft touch-pass to teammate Sue Wicks for an easy layup. After several more smart plays, the Liberty held a 10-point lead with 4:33 left in the first half.

Lobo was not finished. She raised her intensity another notch and single-handedly seized control of the game. She scored her team's next 11 points with an assortment of clever moves. She cut to the basket to take a no-look pass from Coquese Washington to the rack for a layup. She took her defender out to the baseline for a soft 10-footer. She worked free to bank in a pair of short jumpers off the glass. "Rebecca instinctively positions herself very well," said her coach, Nancy Darsch. Lobo capped her incredible scoring run with a fadeaway jumper at the buzzer. The Liberty's 40–21 halftime lead was insurmountable.

"I was just getting the ball a lot in good position," Lobo explained. "Everyone is playing better because we are playing unselfishly and making a lot of passes." Lobo had scored a season-high 17 points against the Sparks earlier in the season in Los Angeles. She had surpassed that total in this game in the first half! It was the kind of play that many had expected of her all along.

When the WNBA debuted a year earlier with the slogan "We Got Next," much of the attention was focused on Lobo. The league is operated by the NBA, and it wanted to generate a positive image from the start. Lobo was an easy choice to be the premier spokeswoman for the league. She is bright and witty and adored by young fans everywhere. She is a six-foot four-inch hardworking forward who plays strong inside and has a soft shooting touch. She was the College Player of the Year in 1995 when she led the University of Connecticut to the national title. She was the youngest member of the 1996 U.S. National Team that won Olympic gold. By then, she had become the ambassador of women's basketball.

"Rebecca Lobo has done more for women's basketball in the nation than anybody," said WNBA vice president Carol Blazejowski. Indeed, with her long braid and easy smile, Lobo was the most recognizable female basketball player in the world. She appeared on television shows such as *The Late Show with David Letterman* and *The Rosie O'Donnell Show*. She played herself in episodes of *Sister Sister, Martin, Mad About You,* and *Sesame Street*.

With her enthusiasm and love for the game, Rebecca Lobo was the perfect spokeswoman for the newly formed WNBA. She soon became the most recognizable women's basketball star in the United States.

In the 1997 season, Lobo routinely led the Liberty in rebounds and blocked shots, even though she was not her team's tallest player. She was a smart passer, a hustling defender, and she took pride in her shooting percentage. Her teammates called her "B." And that is the grade that most would have given her for her play. She was steady, yet unspectacular.

In her second pro season, Lobo's game improved somewhat. She learned to post up and added a skyhook to her game. But expectations of her had risen, as well. People seemed to overlook the fact that she was still just twenty-four years old, still learning, and playing in a league against veteran players, many of whom had gained several years of professional experience overseas. At the season's midpoint, the Liberty had more losses than wins, and Lobo began hearing whispers. She would never be more than a B player, they said. She would never have a pro A game.

To those who knew Lobo, such talk was ridiculous. One shining quality in Lobo's character is that she is a winner. During a stretch that began in college, continued with the national team, and extended to the Liberty, she celebrated 102 straight victories. It was a streak that lasted three years. What other athlete in any sport can match that?

Lobo is Spanish for "wolf." With New York's season on the brink, Lobo raised her intensity level to the ferociousness of a wolf. She was more aggressive in the paint. She became a bigger offensive threat. In the four games prior to the contest with Los Angeles, she hit 28 of 48 shots from the field and averaged nearly 16 points a game. "In the last five weeks," said Coach Darsch, "Rebecca Lobo has really been building on her game. She has been getting better and better."

In the second half of the game against the Sparks, as a national television audience looked on, the Liberty pushed their lead to 31 points before cruising to an 80–62 triumph.

Lobo practices hard so that she will improve. By her second season in the WNBA, her game improved by adding new moves such as the skyhook.

Lobo finished with a season-high 22 points, and also collected 8 rebounds and 2 blocks. Teammates Vickie Johnson and Sophia Witherspoon each had 12 points, while Kym Hampton chipped in with 10. Afterward, all the praise was for Lobo. "B showed her will to be aggressive," said Johnson. "She did it all."

Another of Lobo's qualities is her wondrous sense of humility. She has a sturdy confidence, but she does not need to brag about herself. "Sure, I feel better about how I am playing personally," she said after her brilliant game at Madison Square Garden. "But I think it's more a result of us playing better as a team. I know I am not the type of player that is going to go out there and create my own offense. I am the type of player that has to work within a system. I think as a team we have all grown."

As the Liberty marched toward the playoffs, Lobo's "grade" on the court surely rose. But her perspective on basketball and life, as her true fans can tell you, has always rated an A. Asked what message she thinks the WNBA sends, she says, "When fans watch the women, I think they sense that we play for the love of the game and not for the money. We are also proving that femininity has nothing to do with how much you weigh or how popular you are with boys. You can be an athlete and a woman, too."

When asked what kind of message the WNBA sends to fans, Lobo explained that the women play for fun, and its easy to be an athlete and a woman too.

Chapter 2

Growing Up

From the time she was a young girl, Rebecca Lobo wanted to be a professional athlete. She played many sports and gave special attention to basketball. She was usually the tallest person in her class, and she figured her height would come in handy on the hardwood. She mapped out a plan to become a pro, and she proved that with hard work you can reach your dreams.

Rebecca Rose Lobo was born October 6, 1973, in northern Connecticut. Her parents, Dennis and RuthAnn, had met in college and dated for four years before marrying. They both worked in public education. Dennis was mainly a high school history teacher. RuthAnn was primarily a middle school counselor. This was fortunate because the whole family had the same schedule and same vacation time. They ate dinner together every night and took vacations together every summer.

The Lobos are a tall family. Dennis is six feet five inches, and RuthAnn is five feet eleven inches. It is no wonder that Rebecca grew to be six feet four inches. Her sister, Rachel, who is two years older, is the "shrimp" of the family at five feet ten inches. Her brother, Jason, who

Rebecca is only slightly above average height for someone in her family. When she started playing basketball at age four, she had to face her brother, Jason, who grew to be just less than seven feet.

is four years older than Rebecca and played college basketball at Dartmouth, is just one inch shy of seven feet.

Rebecca lived in Connecticut for her first two years before moving with her family north across the state line to Southwick, Massachusetts. The home where she would spend the rest of her childhood was set by a flat road that wound through a wooded area in which the houses were separated by thickets and groves of trees. A basketball hoop hung above the garage door, and Rebecca describes this area as "a driveway that has had more basketballs bounced on its surface, bikes skidded over it, and skateboards ridden over its bumps than any one person can imagine. This driveway was my whole world while I was growing up."

Rebecca remembers that she played basketball for the first time at age four. She watched her brother, Jason, shoot a rubber basketball through the hoop, and she had to try it, too. "I just wanted to do what he did," she said. But basketball was not the only sport played at the Lobo house. There was whiffle ball, soccer, volleyball, stickball, and even boxing. Jason organized boxing matches between his sisters. "I'd put mittens on them, get on my knees, and referee," said Jason. "If I got them mad enough, they'd box until one of them cried, then I'd spend the next 20 minutes telling them why they couldn't tell Mom." Jason explained to his sisters that telling Mom would be "just too boring."

Jason was usually a very kind brother, however. One time he helped his sisters collect eighteen juice cans and sink them into the backyard lawn so they could have their own miniature golf course. He refereed swimming races between them in the above-ground swimming pool in the backyard. Jason was a sports nut, and he influenced them in this way. When Rebecca was seven, for instance, all she and Rachel wanted for Christmas were football uniforms. Later, when Jason was in high school, he often went to the park to play football with his friends, and he always let his little sisters tag along. He was known on the high school basketball team as the Gentle Giant, and Rebecca liked sitting behind the team's bench so she could hear the conversations among the players. In fourth grade, she and her classmates were asked to write about the person they admired the most. Rebecca chose her brother.

> The person I most admire is not rich or on television; he is my big brother," she wrote. "Jason is who I have always wanted to be like because he is so 'good.' He never fights with me, but he sometimes play fights. He always helps and never disobeys my parents. He will play catch with me. If I am hurt or just feeling down, he will come up to my room, knock on the door, and ask if I am all right. I really love my older brother.

Rebecca's room was filled with stuffed animals and carnival prizes and posters of her favorite athletes. She was able to recite the names of the players for teams like the New York Giants, New England Patriots, and Boston Celtics. In third grade, she found out that her grandmother, Granny Hardy, would be going to a Celtics game. Rebecca wrote a letter for Granny Hardy to give to Celtics general manager Red Auerbach. It read, in part, "I want you to know that I am going to be the first girl to play for the Boston Celtics."

Rebecca had good reason for such confidence. In third grade, she was skilled enough to play on a recreation team of seventh and eighth graders. In fifth grade, there were not enough girls to form a basketball team in Southwick, so Rebecca's mother insisted that her daughter be allowed to play on the boys' team. The boys were skeptical about having a girl play on their team, but Lobo said, "Once I showed them I could play, they were great about it."

Rebecca was a basketball nut, but there were no female

When Rebecca Lobo was young she dreamed of playing professional basketball. At that time the WNBA did not exist, so Rebecca imagined she was the first woman to play for the Boston Celtics.

professional basketball players for her to look up to. The WNBA did not exist until many years later. "Growing up, I remember seeing women in tennis, golf, gymnastics, or figure skating," Lobo says now. "It's exciting because now a lot of girls who play team sports today, like basketball or soccer, can see that their dreams of playing professionally can come true when they get older."

Rebecca attended elementary school in Granby. Her parents stressed the importance of trying her hardest and never giving up. In third grade, for example, Rebecca wanted to quit tap dance lessons. "It was about six weeks before the recital," she said. "I wanted to quit. My mom said, 'No, you're going to stay with it.' Well, I did it, and I was bad, too! But my parents never let their kids walk away from something because it was too hard."

Rebecca's parents always put education ahead of sports. In fourth grade, Rebecca's teacher called to tell Rebecca's parents that their daughter's grades had slipped. "If your grades don't improve," Rebecca's mother told her, "basketball is the first thing to go." Rebecca learned the value of hard work just by being around her parents. "I watched my parents come home from work and do lesson plans and correct papers," she said. "I saw how hard they worked, and that set a good example."

In the school cafeteria at lunchtime, Rebecca's fifth-grade class was assigned two long tables. The girls sat at one table, the boys at the other. Rebecca preferred sitting with the boys. She had plenty of girl friends, but in general, she thought boys had more fun. "The girls were more into hanging around the jungle gym and talking," she said. She never thought there was anything wrong with having friends who were boys. One day, a teacher called Rebecca to her desk to tell her that what she was doing was wrong. Lobo will never forget her teacher's words. "She told me I was too much of a tomboy," said Lobo, "and that I needed

Rebecca learned to be aggressive from playing on many kinds of teams in her youth.

to dress and act more like a girl." Rebecca was stunned. She felt humiliated. She went home and told her parents. Her mother was furious. "We taught our children that everyone has his or her own gifts, talents, and worth," said RuthAnn Lobo. "There is nothing wrong with a girl playing sports and wearing jeans." Rebecca kept playing basketball with the boys at recess against the teacher's wishes, and says her mother might have saved her sports future right then. "It's a good thing my mom's way of thinking was louder in my head than my teacher's," she admitted. "Otherwise, I might have believed there was something wrong with a girl playing basketball."

One day in fifth grade, Rebecca got into trouble. She had passed a note around the room about the substitute teacher that said, "Mrs. M. has a mustache." The substitute teacher saw the note and was very hurt by it. Rebecca felt awful. She was trying to be funny, not mean. The principal sent her home with a note that had to be signed by her parents. Rebecca shot baskets in the driveway and waited for them to come home. "While I was shooting in my driveway that afternoon," Rebecca remembers, "I managed to forget what I had done and that I would be punished. Many people, particularly young kids, need some way to handle the pain or anxiety in their lives. Basketball was my way." When Rebecca's mother read the note, she did not punish Rebecca. Instead, she simply told Rebecca that what she had done was very cruel, and then signed the note. "I learned that day," Rebecca said, "that sometimes you can learn a lesson better when you are not punished than when you are."

By seventh grade at Powdermill Middle School, Rebecca was the tallest person in the entire school. She wore braces on her teeth, and she had what she calls "an out-of-control hairdo." She took sports quite seriously now. During a field hockey game, for instance, Rebecca was whistled for a foul, and she responded by throwing her stick on the ground in disgust. Her mother, who was watching from the sideline, was embarrassed at such a display of poor sportsmanship, especially toward an official. She asked Rebecca about it on the car ride home. "I wasn't mad at the official, Mom," Rebecca said. "I was mad at myself for committing the foul."

Rebecca had become especially focused on basketball now, and by eighth grade she was working out with her brother on a regular basis and attending organized basketball camps. She dreamed of playing professionally. She certainly hoped to play in college. First, however, she had to make the high school team.

Chapter 3

Learning the College Game

At Southwick Tolland Regional High School, Rebecca was an instant basketball star. No one was surprised at this, not even coach James Vincent, who had heard about Rebecca's ability a year earlier from people around town. Coach Vincent had to see her for himself. When Rebecca was still in eighth grade, her sister, Rachel, was a sophomore on the Southwick High team. Coach Vincent asked Rachel one day whether Rebecca would like to play with the team at a weekend Rotary tournament at South Hadley High School. "I remember Rebecca came into the gym with her sneakers slung over her shoulder," Coach Vincent said. "She was tall and gangly out on the court, but she sure knew how to put the ball in the basket." Rebecca was so good, even playing against older girls, that she was named the tournament's Most Valuable Player.

Coach Vincent could not give Rebecca her uniform fast enough. It was green, white, and gold, with jersey number thirty-one. Rebecca stood nearly six feet tall in ninth grade, and she was put at the center position. Immediately she was the center of attention. In her varsity debut against Frontier High School, she scored 32 points in a 56–48 victory. "She was easily our best player," said Coach Vincent. "We had other players who were decent, but she carried the team."

Rebecca's teammates started calling her B. She began wearing her hair in what is now that famous braid, thanks to senior Marcy Vincent, the coach's daughter, who styled it in a braid one day on the bus ride to a game. It became a ritual. Rebecca had her hair put in a braid on the bus for away games, and in the locker room for home games.

With Rebecca leading the way, the Southwick Rams went undefeated through the Bi-County League with a 14–0 record, claiming their first of four straight league titles with her at center. She averaged 22.5 points a game, which was not far off her prep career average of 29.8, and was flooded with honors like All-League, All-Western Massachusetts, *USA Today* All-State, and AAU All-America.

Studying still came first, of course, and Rebecca made the honor roll every year. She even won the principal's award for excellence in social studies and science. She also was a member of the student council and played the saxophone in the school band. In addition to basketball, she also played field hockey all four years, as well as softball for three, before switching to track her senior year. But she loved basketball the most.

Her sophomore year was even better. Besides getting her braces off, she dominated on the court, averaging nearly 27 points a game. She was driven to be the best player she could be. For instance, if she missed a couple of free throws in a game, she stayed afterward, while everyone else left the gym, and shot 50 or more foul shots. Her parents waited in the stands until she said she was ready to

Rebecca began to wear her now-famous braid while playing in high school.

go home. "She really had her goals set up by this point," said Coach Vincent.

Rebecca got a feel for college basketball by traveling with her family to Jason's games at Dartmouth. The Lobos stayed in a motel, with the parents in one bed and the sisters in the other. "The only time we got in each other's way," said Rebecca, "was when everyone wanted a piece of the mirror in the morning."

By her junior year, Rebecca was so dominant under the basket that she was named to Dick Vitale's top 25 squad and the *Parade* All-America team. She hustled on defense and scored over 32 points a game. She was recruited by more than one hundred major colleges, including such powerhouses as Stanford, Virginia, and Penn State. By the end of her junior season, she had become so popular that after every road game she was swarmed for autographs by what seemed like hundreds of kids. The other players would have to wait in the gym or on the bus for her. Sometimes they would urge her to hurry, saying, "C'mon, B, we have to get home. We have school tomorrow."

Rebecca could hardly wait to play in college now, but she stayed on task and kept up with her studies. Her daily routine was school, practice, and then home for homework. She was so focused on her grades now that she was inducted into the National Honor Society. "It's difficult," Lobo tells children now, "but it can be done. You just have to be disciplined and set in your routine."

Rebecca's enchanting senior season began with a single-game high of 62 points on the road against the Ludlow High Lions. "That was an embarrassment for me," she said. "I mean, basketball is a team game." The season ended with the Rams winning their second straight Western Massachusetts Division II championship. In a 51–37 victory over Taconic High at the Springfield Civic Center, Rebecca had 35 points, 25 rebounds, 3 assists, and

9 blocked shots. "Rebecca made some incredible moves out there," said Coach Vincent afterward. "She had a whale of a game." Between her team's first and last victories that year, Rebecca broke the state scoring record. She amassed 2,710 points over her high school career, the highest total in the history of Massachusetts high school basketball, for a girl or a boy. She was the unanimous choice for the State Player of the Year and a finalist for the National Player of the Year.

In the middle of this activity, Rebecca had to choose a college. It was not an easy decision. Stanford is a prestigious school with a fine basketball program, and most people thought this would be her choice. On Wednesday, November 14, 1990, Rebecca made her announcement at a press conference at school in front of the students, teachers, and local newspaper and television reporters. After thanking her teammates, coaches, and family, she said,

> After careful thought and consideration, I have finally come to a decision. I was looking for a school that could offer me the best of both worlds. Strong academics and strong athletics. I needed to feel comfortable with the people on the team, the coaching staff, and the students. There is no doubt that I have made the best decision possible. And I have decided to sign with the University of Connecticut.

UConn coach Geno Auriemma was trying to build a national power. During Rebecca's senior high school year, the Huskies had reached the NCAA Tournament Final Four. Rather than join an established power like Stanford, Rebecca wanted to help build a new one. As a bonus, the Connecticut campus in Storrs was just a one-hour drive south of home. Once she was in college, Rebecca would not go home much on weekends, but knowing that she could gave her comfort.

In her senior year of high school, Rebecca was heavily recruited by many prestigious schools, including Stanford University. In the end, she enrolled at the University of Connecticut.

Lobo was assigned a dormitory room with another freshman basketball player named Pam Webber. The two young women became instant friends, and they stayed roommates all four years in college. Lobo jumped right into her classes, sat up front, took plenty of notes, studied hard, and was even jokingly called a nerd by her teammates.

Lobo found out that she had plenty to learn on the court as well. In her first game, at the University of California, she missed 9 of 12 shots and fouled out after just 26 minutes. She did score 10 points and grab 10 rebounds, but neither she nor her coach felt good about her performance. "When I say she was bad," said Coach Auriemma, "she was bad in just about every aspect of the game." Lobo said simply, "I didn't have a clue what college basketball was about."

Lobo did score 23 points against Louisiana Tech in her third game, but she made plenty of mistakes, too. Sometimes Coach Auriemma yelled at her in practice. Lobo was not used to such treatment. "I didn't understand," she said. "Then again, I was only eighteen years old." In one game, Lobo had a particularly embarrassing moment, when her uniform shorts dropped to her ankles. "I jumped to block a shot against another player, and our bodies got caught," she recalled. "I had forgotten to tie the drawstring, and my shorts fell down! I couldn't believe it! I learned to tie a drawstring after that."

Lobo's parents attended every home game at Gampel Pavilion, and they watched their daughter grow more comfortable on the court. Against St. John's University, Lobo scored a season-high 29 points. Against Providence, she dominated in the paint with 18 points and 18 rebounds. She finished the season with impressive averages of 14.3 points and 7.9 rebounds a game, and she was honored as the Big East Rookie of the Year. In the sixty-four-team NCAA Tournament, the Huskies beat St. Peter's in the opening round before losing to Vanderbilt. UConn finished with a 23–11 record.

In the summer before her sophomore year, and every summer after that, Lobo stayed on campus to take summer school classes so that she could take fewer courses during the basketball season. Her favorite thing to do during these quiet summer months was to go to Gampel Pavilion in the morning, close the door, and practice alone. The only sounds she heard were her squeaking sneakers and the rhythmic thumping of the basketball as she dribbled— wump . . . wump . . . wump. Her mind often wandered away like a soft summer breeze.

Trouble came her sophomore year. Many of the players from the Final Four team two years earlier had graduated. Several more players suffered early-season injuries, and another quit. Most of the season there were just eight players able to play. The team could not even hold full-court scrimmages in practice. The weight was squarely on Lobo's shoulders now. She had to be on the floor in games nearly all the time. She was always double-teamed. Sometimes she had three defenders on her. Opponents banged hard on her and tried to wear her down. "Generally this sort of responsibility and pressure doesn't come until you're a junior or senior," she lamented. "It knocked on my door when I was a sophomore."

Coach Auriemma yelled at Lobo to get tougher, to bang harder, to get meaner. Lobo did not like the yelling. She felt tremendous pressure. She grew to resent the coach. She felt "mistreated and misunderstood." She dreaded going to practice. The Huskies were 7–3, but Lobo played inconsistently. She was great one night, average the next. And she was miserable. Coach Auriemma was frustrated, too, and he finally said, "We're at a crossroads. I can't reach you. If you want to leave, fine. Or you stay here, and I'll leave."

Rebecca Lobo had a lot to learn in her first season of college basketball. Still, she triumphed and earned the Big East Rookie of the Year Award.

One night Associate Head Coach Chris Dailey insisted on driving Lobo and her roommate, Pam Webber, to Coach Auriemma's house to "clear the air." The coach explained to Lobo that he coached a certain way and that she had to adjust to it. Lobo said nothing, but on the car ride home, she complained to Coach Dailey. "Well, why didn't you tell him all that?" asked Coach Dailey. Lobo was respectful of authority, but she realized that in this case, she was intimidated. She decided to try again to talk with Coach Auriemma, so she met him the next day in his office. Lobo told her coach that she was uncomfortable with his yelling. He listened. Then he explained how frustrated he was. He said that he was trying to get her to focus better. If she played well one game and poorly the next, he explained, the problem could only be concentration. It was not her skills that were holding her back from being consistently great, but her head: "As soon as I understood that he was simply trying to get the most out of me," Lobo said, "my anger disappeared. My mind cleared. A change in our relationship occurred that day."

In February 1993, defending national champion Stanford came to Storrs to beat the Huskies, 68–54. Lobo scored 10 points and grabbed 14 rebounds in the game. She was disappointed with the loss, but excited about something else. This was the first sellout ever at Gampel Pavilion, and the attendance figure of 8,241 was a record for the Big East. The game also was broadcast live on CBS and had high ratings. It marked a turning point in the popularity of women's college basketball. A month later, in the opening round of the NCAA Tournament, UConn's season ended in a 74–71 loss to Louisville.

Lobo vowed that her junior year would be different. It certainly started out that way. With Pam Webber and Jennifer Rizzotti at guard, Lobo and Jamelle Elliott at forward, and six-foot seven-inch freshman Kara Wolters at center, the Huskies had a strong lineup. Lobo and Wolters dominated in the middle from the start, and together they became known as the Twin Towers.

In early December, UConn pulled an upset win at home against powerhouse Auburn, 64–55. Lobo led the way with 19 points and 14 rebounds. Three nights later, at Gampel Pavilion, the Huskies beat mighty Virginia, 74–63, in a spirited affair. "It was the moment that I first heard a crowd go wild while I was playing," said Lobo, who had 20 points and 15 rebounds. When the final buzzer sounded, she raised her arms in triumph. "I'd had a great night," she said. "I was having the best basketball week of my life." After the game, Lobo talked to reporters and then signed autographs for fans as her parents stood off to the side. When the last autograph had been signed, Lobo's mother approached her and said, "I have something I need to tell you." The grim look on RuthAnn's face told Rebecca that something was wrong. Together they walked up into the stands and sat down in Section 109. RuthAnn began to talk. Rebecca listened. Suddenly she was crying.

Chapter 4

Road to the Final Four

Rebecca's mother had cancer. She needed to have surgery immediately. Even then, there was no guarantee how things would turn out. "Don't cry," RuthAnn Lobo said. "I don't want you worrying about me. You do what you have to do, and I'll do what I have to do. The best thing you and the family can do is continue your daily lives."

The other players on the team were informed of RuthAnn's condition, but were told to keep it a secret. Meanwhile, Lobo's world had been turned upside down. "I was shocked," she said. "I never thought this could happen to my mother." She prayed every day for her mother, and she found the inner strength to continue. "I kept playing basketball and studying," she said, "but things got worse." During Christmas break, Lobo and her mother went to the doctor's office, where they were given more bad news. The cancer had spread. Chemotherapy treatments were needed at once. Rebecca started crying again.

RuthAnn Lobo began undergoing chemotherapy treatments. The drugs made her very sick, but she refused to miss a single game at UConn. One night she showed up wearing a wig. The drugs had made her hair fall out. She was determined to see her daughter play, no matter what. "She would be sick as a dog some days, and still make it to the game," said Lobo. "She said it was kind of like her therapy. It was kind of her way to escape."

Lobo found herself glancing up in the stands every so often to sneak a peek at her mother. Mostly, though, she kept her concentration on the court, and she played at both ends of the floor with relentless abandon. She set personal highs for points, rebounds, and blocks, and averaged more than 19 points and 4 blocks a game. She shot a reliable 54.6 percent from the field and 73.8 percent from the line. She was selected the Big East Player of the Year and named to the All-America team. More important to her was her team, which finished with a brilliant 27–2 regular season record and the Big East title.

At the Big East Tournament awards banquet at a hotel ballroom in Hartford, Connecticut, Lobo thanked her coaches, teammates, and fans, and then, all of a sudden, she was gripped with emotion. "This," she said, holding the trophy and choking back tears, "is for my mother. She has been the real competitor this year, and this is for her." Lobo told the public about her mother's battle with cancer. The media reported the story the next day, and suddenly RuthAnn and Rebecca were flooded with mail from people across the country. They were overwhelmed by the support and replied to as many letters as they could.

The Huskies were among the top four seeds in the NCAA Tournament, and for the first three rounds, they played that way. They beat Brown, Auburn, and Southern Mississippi to reach the Great Eight. They were one win away from the famed Final Four. But on March 26, at the Rutgers Athletic Center, they were upset by North Carolina, 81–69. Lobo had yearned to reach the Final Four

Lobo had some personal difficulties during her junior year of college. Friends and teammates such as Pam Webber helped her stay focused on her game.

at least once in her college career, and this loss was devastating. She was down to one chance. "We can't let this feeling go away," she said after the game. "We have to keep a piece with us because this is what's going to drive us to work hard this summer and fall."

Rebecca Lobo spent the next few weeks responding to as many letters from fans as she could. Meanwhile, RuthAnn Lobo completed her chemotherapy treatments with wonderful success. Her cancer disappeared. It has been in remission ever since. The whole terrifying experience changed Lobo's outlook forever. "I learned to appreciate how precious life is," she said. "I learned how to enjoy small things, like a sunset or the changing of the leaves. I don't let the little things upset me anymore."

Lobo's senior season was magical. It was redemption for all the tournament losses as well as a personal assault on the record books. It began with a victory by 80 points, and the 107–27 victory over Morgan State was not the only blowout for the Huskies. Against California, they started the game with a 25–0 lead. They beat Iona, 101–42, as Lobo took 11 shots and made them all. They beat Providence, 104–50. They won all 35 of their games, and they won them by an average of 35 points. As Anne Flannery, a director for Spalding Sports Worldwide, described it, "Rebecca is a phenomenon. Cheryl Miller had her day; she took women's basketball to another level. Then Sheryl Swoopes took it one step farther. But no one else has had the combination of dynamics that Rebecca and the UConn team enjoyed."

The Huskies were 12–0 midway through the season and ranked No. 2 in the Associated Press poll behind Tennessee when the mighty Volunteers arrived in Connecticut. A huge television audience tuned in to ESPN to watch. Gampel Pavilion was packed with 8,241 cheering fans, some of them paying as much as $100 for a ticket that

The 1995 season for UConn was magical. With Lobo's help, they won all 35 of their regular season games by an average of 35 points.

usually sold for $8. Lobo and her teammates were nervous at first, but Jennifer Rizzotti pulled them together at the free-throw line five minutes into it and screamed, "We are going to win this game!" Lobo said that was all it took to send her "flying." The Huskies gained control to take a 41–33 lead into the locker room at halftime.

In the second half, the crowd took over. "They simply did not let us lose the game," said Lobo. "They stood in their seats, screamed, clapped, hollered, and did anything else they could to make noise." UConn won, 77–66, as Lobo scored 13 points and led her team with 8 rebounds and 5 blocks. Kara Wolters finished with 18 points, Rizzotti had 17, and Jamelle Elliott and Nykesha Sales added 12 each. "I've never had an experience like this game," Lobo said afterward. "Seeing the fans jumping up and down and hugging each other because their team had won defined for me what sports is all about."

The AP poll was released the next day, and it was official. UConn was ranked No. 1 for the first time since the poll had begun nineteen years earlier. "Huskymania" was in full bloom now, and Lobo, with her long braid, had become among the most recognizable female athletes in the country. "Anything with Rebecca Lobo on it sells," said a merchandising official at Gampel Pavilion. One day a fan saw Lobo getting a haircut in a salon. The fan ran in and scooped up some of Lobo's hair from the floor and put it in a bag as a souvenir. "The attention is flattering," said Lobo. "But it can get weird."

The only real test for the Huskies before the NCAA Tournament came on the road in late January at the Kemper Arena against seventeenth-ranked Kansas. In front of 16,981 fans, which was the largest crowd ever to see a UConn game to that point, as well as a national television audience, the Huskies passed the test with a 97–87 triumph. Lobo led the way with a season-high 25 points, along with 12 rebounds.

Rebecca Lobo had become a national heroine. At Villanova in late February, as she stood on the court after the game to be interviewed, security guards had to surround her and push back the crush of young admirers. After a game at Syracuse, she was mobbed by young girls seeking autographs and stood for an hour signing her name. "It was Girl Scout Day," said Syracuse coach Marianna Freeman, "and there were over one thousand Brownies and Girl Scouts in our stands. For Rebecca to do what she did—those little girls will remember it for a long time."

When Lobo's parents escorted her onto the court for Senior Night at Gampel Pavilion, a tremendous cheer rang out for RuthAnn Lobo, in honor of her courage in her battle against cancer. Afterward, Rebecca Lobo had 13 points and 16 rebounds to lead the Huskies to a 103–56 thumping of St. John's. Two weeks later, they pounded Seton Hall, 85–49, to win the Big East Championship. It capped a regular season that was absolutely perfect—almost. The only slip-up occurred in Washington, D.C., after a victory over Georgetown. The team had assembled for a planned tour of the White House and a chance to meet President Clinton. They stood outside a specified gate at a certain time as they were instructed to do. But because of a foul-up, the gate never opened, and they had to go home.

Lobo finished as Connecticut's all-time leader in rebounding and blocked shots, but just as pleasing to her was making the dean's list for excellent grades her last two years. She graduated with a degree in political science and was named to the Academic All-America Team. She was also the consensus Naismith National Player of the Year. Despite such grand success, however, she knew she would not feel ultimate joy unless her team won the NCAA Tournament title. It would take six straight wins to do it.

The Huskies opened with a 105–75 win against Maine, and followed with a 91–45 victory over Virginia Tech. In the East Regional Final, they rolled over Alabama, 87–56. In the Regional Final against Virginia, they jumped out to a 29–10 run in the first 10 minutes, and they seemed destined for the Minneapolis and the Final Four. But then the Huskies got the scare of their life. The Cavaliers outscored them, 34–8, to close out the first half. The Huskies trailed by seven points at halftime, marking the first time all season they were behind at that point. Would their dream of a perfect season turn into a nightmare? Lobo had been double-teamed underneath, and she was forcing up shots. In the locker room, Coach Auriemma told her to rely on her defense. Lobo stepped up to the challenge. She blocked 6 shots, the last coming with 52 seconds left and UConn clinging to a three-point lead. The Huskies prevailed, 67–63, and were on their way to the Final Four.

Only one women's college basketball team had ever gone undefeated through a season—the Longhorns of Texas nine years earlier. Connecticut was two games from matching the feat, but most experts predicted that Tennessee would beat them in the title game. First the Huskies had to get there. They met Stanford in the semifinal, and before the game, Coach Auriemma told Lobo, "Don't try to prove you're the Player of the Year. Let the game come to you." It was sound advice. Lobo played relaxed and had a solid 17 points and 9 rebounds to carry the Huskies to an easy 87–60 victory. Meanwhile, Tennessee blew out Georgia, 73–51, in the other semifinal to set the stage for the championship game. Said Stanford coach Tara VanDerveer, "Tennessee is going to win tomorrow, but I think it will be a good game."

Over eighteen thousand fans, including RuthAnn and

Dennis Lobo, filled the Target Center for the 1995 title game. Back in Connecticut, more people watched this game than the Super Bowl. Lobo found out early that she would have her hands full against Tennessee's big inside power, six-foot four-inch Tiffani Johnson and six-foot six-inch Vonda Ward. Just eight minutes into the first half, Lobo committed her third personal foul and had to go to the bench (college players have to leave the game once they get five fouls). Jennifer Rizzotti joined her on the bench a few minutes later with her third personal. The situation looked bleak for the Huskies. They trailed, 31–25, and their two senior leaders were saddled with foul trouble. Still, Coach Auriemma managed to slow down the game and keep the deficit at six, 38–32, at halftime.

With UConn's big guns back on the floor for the second half, the Huskies tried to stage a comeback. But the Lady Vols kept hitting key baskets to maintain their lead. With 11:32 left and the Huskies still trailing by six, 52–46, Kara Wolters committed her fourth foul and had to leave the game. Lobo knew she had to take over the game now, or it would be too late. She had scored just 6 points. She told her teammates to get her the ball. And then she took over. First she took the ball inside and made a nifty post-up move to score on a layup. After a steal and pass by Jamelle Elliott, Lobo drove the lane and scored on a reverse layup, cutting the lead to 52–50.

Tennessee jumped back ahead by five, but Lobo responded by draining a clutch 18-foot jumper from the left wing. The Vols answered with a layup, but Lobo nailed a 17-footer from the perimeter to cut the lead to three. Rizzotti followed with a steal and layup to get the Huskies to within one point, 58–57, with seven minutes left. Elliott gave UConn the lead with a pair of free throws with 5:44 to go. Tennessee reclaimed the lead a minute later with a three-point play. Elliott's layup tied the game, 61–61, with

When the buzzer sounded at the end of the NCAA Title game, Lobo ran up and down the court shouting with joy. Here, she and Coach Auriemma hold the NCAA National Championship Trophy.

2:17 left. Rizzotti took a long rebound coast-to-coast for a layup to give the Huskies a 63–61 lead with 1:51 left. After that, the Huskies iced the game at the free-throw line, hitting seven of eight attempts. Three of those free throws were by Lobo. All the time she had spent practicing free throws after games in the high school gym had paid off. The Huskies won the national title, 70–64. Lobo had scored 11 of her team's final 18 points to will the Huskies to victory.

At the sound of the buzzer, Lobo ran the length of the court out of sheer madness. She turned around and saw her teammates jumping and hugging in the middle of the court, and she took off after them and joined the crazy celebration. She called it "a picture-perfect way for someone to end her career." She was named the Most Valuable Player of the Final Four, and humbly stepped from the spotlight, saying, "We didn't have the best basketball players or the best basketball team in the country. We just had a team that worked incredibly well together." She found out later that dozens of people were honoring her at that moment back in Connecticut by playing basketball in her driveway. With a telephone call to the locker room, President Clinton invited the Huskies to the White House Rose Garden. Coach Auriemma thanked the president, then joked, "Maybe this time we'll come through the front door."

Chapter 5

From Olympian to Pro

Artist Andy Warhol once said, "In the future, everyone will be famous for fifteen minutes." Lobo knew that famous quotation, and was referring to it when she said, "I'm just waiting for the timer to buzz and my 15 minutes will be over." She could not know that her "fifteen minutes" would last years.

Lobo flew home to Connecticut with her team and was greeted at the airport by thousands of fans. Within weeks, her rise to fame was chronicled in nearly every magazine in the country. The WNBA did not yet exist, and Lobo figured that in order to play professionally, she would have to join a league in Europe. "It's a little frustrating," she said, "but I'm thankful that I can get paid at all just to continue playing this game." In the meantime, she took her college final exams, and on the day after her last test, she flew to the Olympic Training Center in Colorado Springs to try to win a spot on the U.S. National Team that would play the following summer in the Olympic Games.

Because of her stellar play and hard work at UConn, Lobo earned a spot on the United States Olympic Team. She was the youngest member of the squad.

Lobo made the team. She was the youngest of a ten-member squad that would travel around and the world to prepare for the Olympics. She joined veteran stars like Teresa Edwards and Katrina McClain, who had been playing professionally in Europe. She and her teammates were paid a salary of about $50,000 by the Olympic Committee. Lobo would not be the star of the national team, or even a starter, but she did play, and she learned plenty of new moves.

The U.S. team opened in the fall with a twenty-game national tour against the best college competition, including a game at Gampel Pavilion against Connecticut. As Lobo sat on the visitors' bench and listened to the crowd cheer for the Huskies, she felt an odd sense of torn loyalty. "At the beginning of the game, I said, 'Is it bad when I feel happy when UConn does good things?'" she said. "A big piece of my heart is still with this team." Once she was on the court, the game felt more like a practice to Lobo. She knew her ex-teammates' moves, and they knew hers. Kara Wolters blocked one of Lobo's shots. Lobo responded with 8 points in 13 minutes of playing time as the national team rolled to an easy 83–47 win.

During this tour and then the world tour that followed, Lobo carried around a laptop computer. Rebecca and RuthAnn Lobo had been given a contract by a publishing company to write a book about their lives called The Home Team. Rebecca said that writing the book was "a challenge," and joked that it was the longest thing she had written since the words "I won't talk in class" in elementary school.

The U.S. team traveled from country to country, winning every game it played. Each player kept a picture of the gold medal in her gym bag as a reminder of the ultimate goal. The Americans staged stirring comebacks, beating both Canada and Russia to keep their winning streak alive.

When they finally returned home, they had compiled a record of 52–0. It was great fun for Lobo. The only thing she regretted was missing out again on meeting the president. While she was in Europe, the Huskies finally got to visit the White House. But Lobo would meet the president soon enough.

Lobo's focus at the moment was on the Olympics. The 1996 Summer Games were staged in Atlanta, Georgia, and the American women's basketball team was a heavy favorite to win the gold. "We're not worried about other people's expectations because no one's could be higher than our own," Lobo said. "Our goal is to win a gold medal. We feel if we play the best we can, we can achieve that." Winning the gold medal was a breeze for the Americans. They rolled through eight opponents, including Brazil in the gold medal game, to become Olympic champions. Lobo did not play much, averaging just 4 points and 2 rebounds. But one year after becoming a college national champion, she was now an Olympic champion, and she had the gold medal around her neck to prove it.

Finally, Lobo got to meet the president. President Clinton invited her to jog with him. Her brother, Jason, was invited, too. They flew to Washington, D.C., drove to the White House, and suddenly found themselves climbing into a limousine with the president. They rode with a police escort in front and behind to the site of their jog. "He chatted with us the whole time," said Lobo. "The more he spoke, the more comfortable I felt." She never noticed the secret service agents with binoculars that lined the riverbank. As they started their jog, Lobo stayed behind the president. She was careful not to get too close for fear of accidentally tripping him. Toward the end of the jog, President Clinton waved to her to come up alongside him. Media photographers clicked away. There they went,

In 1996 the WNBA was formed. Lobo was assigned to the New York Liberty, along with teammate Teresa Weatherspoon.

elbow to elbow down the path, President Clinton and Rebecca Lobo. Her fifteen minutes of fame were still ticking along.

The spotlight on Lobo was about to become permanent. More than one hundred years earlier, in 1892, Senda Berenson Abbott had formed the first organized women's basketball team, at Smith College, in Northampton, Massachusetts. The signs posted outside the gymnasium read: "Men Are Not Permitted To Watch." The women wore long dresses. A century later, women's pro basketball in the United States still had not taken hold. Throughout the years, several pro leagues had been formed, but all of them collapsed due to the lack of public interest. Finally, in the middle of the last decade of the twentieth century, it appeared as though enough Americans had finally recognized the excitement of the women's game to support a league. Why did the interest come now? Rebecca Lobo and the excitement generated by the 1995 college champion Connecticut Huskies deserve as much credit as anyone.

The American Basketball League (ABL) opened for business in 1995. A year later, the WNBA was formed. Suddenly there were two leagues, but not for long. The ABL had plenty of stars, but it did not have the money to compete with the upstart WNBA, which would be supported initially by the successful NBA. The ABL folded in 1998, and its players joined the ranks of the WNBA. The new league began play in the summer of 1997.

This meant everything to Lobo. She would not have to go overseas to play professionally. What's more, she was about to find out that she would be playing near home. On January 23, 1997, Lobo was "assigned" to the New York Liberty. Each of the eight teams was assigned two players, according to that player's regional ties. Since Lobo was a college star in the Northeast, assigning her to the Liberty was an easy choice. "I'm excited to be playing in Madison Square Garden," said an elated Lobo. "It's one of the most storied arenas in sports. I'm looking forward to that first game."

The average salary of a WNBA player that first year was about $30,000. Since Lobo was a star, however, she received a contract for about $250,000. She also signed endorsement contracts with companies such as General Motors and Spalding, which raised her income to over half a million dollars. Reebok even named a shoe "The Lobo" and made a TV commercial about it. Lobo spread around her wealth as best she could. New York Liberty coach Nancy Darsch sometimes saw the players show up for practice with new sneakers, and the coach would ask, "Where'd you get the kicks?" The players would answer, "B hooked us up."

There was great anticipation over the new league. Outside the Reebok Sports Club on Columbus Avenue in Manhattan where the Liberty practiced, fans gathered to catch a glimpse of Lobo. "There is pressure on her," said Liberty general manager Carol Blazejowski. "But Rebecca is wise beyond her years. Is she the best athlete in the league? Absolutely not. But she's one of the smartest."

WNBA games would be broadcast on three networks: NBC, ESPN, and Lifetime.

League officials projected that the teams would average about four thousand fans a game. It turned out that women's basketball was far more popular than they predicted. Average attendance the first year was nearly ten thousand. At Madison Square Garden, the Liberty averaged 13,270. "We were hoping for five thousand," said Lobo. It was clear that the time for professional women's basketball in the United States had finally arrived. Everyone knew that the popularity of Rebecca Lobo had much to do with it. "Rebecca was an incredible ambassador at a time when we badly needed one," said WNBA president Val Ackerman. "The league owes her a lot."

There was still the matter of playing the games. On June 21, 1997, the WNBA tipped off its schedule with a game between the New York Liberty and the Los Angeles Sparks. It was billed as a matchup between Lobo and Sparks superstar veteran Lisa Leslie. Most figured Leslie would dominate young Lobo. "I don't feel like I have anything to prove," said Lobo. "I don't know who I'll be guarding, and I don't know who'll be guarding me. I just have to go out there and play and get my offense going." Lobo did just that, scoring 16 points to lead her team to victory.

Lobo turned in other solid performances early in the season, such as grabbing 8 offensive rebounds against the Charlotte Sting. She helped the Liberty win their first seven games. On July 7, the Liberty were beaten by the Phoenix Mercury. It meant only one loss in the standings, but for Lobo, it was her first defeat in over three years. Her amazing streak of combined college, pre-Olympic, Olympic, and pro victories had ended at 102 games.

The loss seemed to rattle the Liberty, who lost again two nights later to the last-place Sting, 87–69. Lobo declared that this losing had to stop. The next night, back in New York, the Liberty gained revenge with a 62–48 win over the Sting. Lobo scored 10 first-half points to lead the way and finished with a team-high 16.

The Liberty battled through July for first place in the Eastern Division. Lobo had been playing her usual steady game. She was averaging more than 13 points and 8 rebounds a game. But she knew that many people saw her as the darling of the WNBA. She began to feel that she was not doing enough to live up to her image. The truth was, she was still just twenty-three years old, much younger than

With Lobo's help, the Liberty battled for first place in the Eastern Division in the 1997 season. That year, Lobo also began to feel the pressure of being a "superstar."

most of the other players. But she started pressing and trying to do more. She took shots from longer range than she was used to. She began missing more. Soon she started hearing an occasional boo from the stands. "People expected me to get 20 points a night," she said. "I wasn't given time to develop."

Lobo and Coach Nancy Darsch had several talks. The coach convinced Lobo to play within herself and be patient. Slowly Lobo's natural game began to return. It blossomed one night in August against the Utah Starzz when she had 9 rebounds and 5 blocks and sizzled the net with 11 baskets, including three three-pointers, for a career-high 27 points. Still, the Liberty lost seven of their final nine regular season games, including their last five on the road. New York finished one game behind the Houston Comets.

The Liberty's 17–11 record was still good enough to make the playoffs. But they had to play their semifinal game on the road where they were having trouble winning. Even worse, they had to play the Phoenix Mercury at America West Arena, which was considered the loudest atmosphere for a WNBA game. Sure enough, 16,751 fans who packed the arena screamed so loudly that the Liberty often could not hear the play-calling of point guard Teresa Weatherspoon. New York managed to hold a slim 23–18 lead at the half. Then Lobo took over. She scored seven quick points, and the Liberty opened the second half with a 17–8 run that gave them a 40–26 lead and quieted the crowd. Lobo finished with 16 points, 9 rebounds, 4 assists, 3 blocks, and 3 steals as New York cruised to a 59–41 victory. "We wanted to do something special," Lobo told reporters. "We played a great game under pressure. People can say what they want about me and about our team, but we're going to the championship. That's all that matters now."

Against the Houston Comets in the title game, the Liberty could not find a way to stop Cynthia Cooper. The league's MVP scored 15 points and directed her offense to a 65–51 victory. Lobo was disappointed not to win the title, but she could not help feeling thrilled about the success of this new league. In addition to the 16,751 fans who packed the Summit in Houston, the game was telecast to more than 165 countries around the world. It was now clear to Lobo that the WNBA was here to stay.

Chapter 6

Team Player

Rebecca Lobo's popularity had skyrocketed, and she spent much of her time now going around the country speaking to groups. She was making a public appearance at a banquet one day when a college student raised her hand and asked, "How hard of an adjustment was it to go from being a superstar in college to an average player in the WNBA?" People in the audience shifted uncomfortably in their seats. Lobo smiled and said, "That is a great question. Let me repeat it so everyone can hear. How hard was it to go from being a superstar in college to an above-average player in the WNBA?" The audience roared with laughter.

The truth is, Lobo has yet to become a true WNBA "superstar." But she never claimed to be. She is a hard-working force inside, a heady defender, a smart and unselfish passer, and a good shooter. She is the consummate team player. She may not score 30 points every game, but she does what she can to help her team win, because winning is more important to her than her own statistics.

Lobo led her team in rebounds and blocks and was second in scoring in 1997, and she was named to the

All-WNBA Second Team. In 1998 she repeated those accomplishments. But when the team struggled early in its second season, losing four of its first five games, her expression on the court showed how much she cared. As she explained later, "I think people watch me to see a joy in the game. When the Liberty were struggling early, I got letters that said, 'We aren't disappointed because you're losing, or because of how you're playing. We're disappointed because you aren't smiling.'"

New York won four straight games in June and six straight toward the end of the season, to finish with an 18–12 record. But this time the Liberty missed the playoffs by one game. From a marketing standpoint, though, the team was an even bigger success than in its debut season. The Liberty averaged 14,935 per game at the Garden. Jerseys and other merchandise with Lobo's name on them were among the top-selling items in the league.

As Lobo headed into the 1999 season, she seemed determined to establish her place in the WNBA order. She knew she was above average, but she believed this was her time to be more than that. "People have to understand what my game is," she explained. "It's not all about numbers, there's a bigger picture here. I'm not Cynthia Cooper or Sheryl Swoopes. I don't create off the dribble. I rely on my teammates. My role is to set screens and get rebounds. But you know what? In the next three years, I will be one of the best players in the league."

Then disaster struck. In the 1999 season opener at Madison Square Garden against the Cleveland Rockers, Lobo suffered a devastating injury. It happened just forty-two seconds into the game. On New York's second possession, Kym Hampton missed a shot, and Lobo skied for the rebound. She grabbed the ball and came down with it. Her knee twisted awkwardly, and she crumpled to the floor. Players huddled around her under the basket, and

During the opening game of the 1999 season Rebecca suffered a devastating knee injury. She was out for the entire 1999 and 2000 seasons.

then the team trainer helped her to the locker room. She was taken to the hospital for tests to determine the extent of the injury. Doctors confirmed the worst. The anterior cruciate ligament in Rebecca's left knee had been torn. She needed surgery to repair it. She would be lost for the season. "To know Rebecca isn't here is an awful feeling," said teammate Teresa Weatherspoon. "Every girl will pick it up for Rebecca."

Lobo officially played exactly one minute of the 1999 season. Despite her season-ending injury, fans voted her as a starter for the inaugural WNBA All-Star Game. She could not play, of course, but she was touched by the support of the fans. As the Liberty continued on with their season, Lobo went every day to a weight room for physical therapy. She lifted weights and performed a variety of stretches to strengthen the knee. At Liberty games, she sat on the bench in street clothes, yearning for the day when she could return. Six months later, while gearing up for the 2000 season by performing some simple basketball drills,

Even though she was unable to play, Rebecca went to every Liberty game, sitting on the bench cheering for her teammates. Behind the scenes Rebecca went through intensive physical therapy to heal her injured knee.

she suffered another setback when she reinjured the same knee. Doctors had to perform surgery again. "We are devastated," said Liberty general manager Carol Blazejowski. "But I am confident that Rebecca will work even harder to come back from this stronger and even more competitive than ever."

In February 1999 a locker honoring Lobo was put on display in the Naismith Basketball Hall of Fame. She was told that her locker at the museum should be a reflection of herself. So Lobo put some things in a box and mailed them to the Hall of Fame. Among other items, she sent an assortment of jerseys and basketball shoes from UConn, the Olympic Team, and the Liberty; a trading card of her favorite NBA player—San Antonio Spurs center David Robinson; a copy of her favorite book, *This Present Darkness*, by Frank E. Peretti; a CD of religious music, *Gonna Need a Hand*, by singer Sean Forest; and some Juicy Fruit gum.

As Lobo works her knee back into shape and prepares to rejoin the New York Liberty, she takes time to think about how much she cares about children. She still thinks and acts like a kid, too, of course. She still likes to eat cookies 'n' cream ice cream and watch Roadrunner cartoons. But she often realizes how lucky she is to be able to send positive messages to children through basketball. "When you come to our games," says Lobo, "what's really exciting is not just girls asking for our autographs but boys. As I see it, if a boy asks for my autograph, maybe he will treat a girl his age differently or look at her differently. Maybe he will pick her to play on his basketball team, or pick her for soccer in gym class, and realize that girls can be pretty good athletes too."

Rebecca Lobo's message to children is this: "Be a good person and study hard. Don't do drugs. Treat other people, no matter who they are, with respect and dignity and fairness. Remember that even if opportunities aren't there now, that doesn't mean they won't be there next year or five years from now. Have goals and dreams. I've had so many dreams come true in my life. Don't be embarrassed to have dreams."

Many of Lobo's dreams have come true because of her intense determination. Her advice to young people is simple, "Don't be embarrassed to have dreams."

Career Statistics

College

Year	Team	GP	FG%	FT%	REB	AST	BLK	PTS	PPG
1991–92	Connecticut	29	.494	.701	228	26	46	416	14.3
1992–93	Connecticut	29	.449	.647	326	37	97	484	16.7
1993–94	Connecticut	33	.546	.738	371	68	131	635	19.2
1994–95	Connecticut	35	.500	.675	343	129	122	598	17.1
Totals		126	.498	.695	1,268	260	396	2,133	16.9

WNBA

Year	Team	GP	FG%	FT%	REB	AST	BLK	PTS	PPG
1997	New York	28	.376	.610	203	53	51	348	12.4
1998	New York	30	.484	.710	207	44	33	350	11.7
1999	New York	1	—	—	1	0	0	0	—
2000	DID NOT PLAY—INJURED								
Totals		59	.430	.660	411	97	84	698	11.8

GP=Games Played   **AST**=Assists   **PTS**=Points Scored
FG%=Field Goal Percentage   **FT%**=Free Throw Percentage   **REB**=Rebounds
BLK=Blocks   **PPG**=Points Per Game

Where to Write Rebecca Lobo:

Rebecca Lobo
c/o New York Liberty
Two Pennsylvania Plaza
New York, NY 10121

On the Internet at:

http://www.wnba.com/playerfile/rebecca_lobo.html
http://www.wnba.com/rebeccalobo/

Index